PENNY TOOGOOD

Fearless

Finding hope for life in uncertain times

Contents

Preface

No matter what is going on in life or where we find ourselves on any given day there is one that remains a constant through it all.

The word tells us that Jesus is the same yesterday, today and forever.

When everything else looks uncertain and when we struggle to hold on we can simply let go of all our striving and efforts and rest assured that the one who created the universe and holds it in his hand is holding onto us.

Throughout scripture we are reminded to " fear not." Jesus himself in his last words to his disciples encouraged them to " not let their hearts be troubled and to not be afraid."

In a world that is living on a constant diet fear and dread about the future I believe that the God of the whole universe is calling us to look to him and to live life fearlessly

Join us each day and let the Lord remind you of his hope for your life.

1

Can you take God at his word?

*S*end men to spy out the land of Canaan, which I am giving to the people of Israel. From each tribe of their fathers you shall send a man, every one a chief among them."

Numbers 13:2

If you're a parent you will probably be very familiar with the trauma of saying goodbye to your child on their first day at school. As a former primary school teacher I was used to the start of a new year with tearful kids & sometimes parents. Some run into school not even looking behind them while others would be clinging to their Mums or Dads at the door. However, no matter how much you know the drill and how quickly you have seen kids settle down and content themselves, you are still left with that ache in your heart and lump in your throat when it's your turn. How can you convince them that you will come back? How can you get them to understand that you would never do anything that would ever harm them?

As loving parents we would never bring pain or suffering into their lives, our intentions towards them are always for their good. So how much more does our loving Heavenly Father want us to know and understand this truth when it comes to how he will lead and guide us everyday.

In today's verse we see the Lord speaking to the children of Israel. He makes a promise to them about their future. He has just delivered them from 400 years of slavery and now he is about to show what He has in store for them.

He is sending spies out into the land to give them a vision of what they are about to inherit. He is not taking them there to show them an incredible land and then allow them to be destroyed by the inhabitants. What kind of a Father would do that? Who would set their children up to fail? This would be the antithesis of what love looks like. And yet we know from the story that although God makes this declaration that He will give them this land, the spies struggle to believe it to be true. In fact 10 of the 12 come back with a bad report. They recognise that the land is a good land "flowing with milk and honey´ but their enthusiasm for the land pales away when they see the size of the people living there. They do not see that God has used these strong giants to do all the hard labour of building cities and cultivating the land. They can't see the potential of what life could look like! All they can see is their inability to be able to overcome! They are filled with fear!

And yet they had not left Egypt because of their brute strength or their cunning plans. They had escaped Egypt by the hand of the Lord and by following his ways. Why would this next step in the journey be any different?

This is why it is so important to remember. To look back, to recall what God has done. To carry around in our hearts the stories of his goodness, his love, his protection, his faithfulness and his deliverance. How often do we find ourselves in trying situations and we forget what God has already done. We allow the giants to overshadow us and we suddenly believe we are at the mercy of the world's system or the schemes of the enemy. We are afraid and fearful for the future.

Don't be like the children of Israel who ended up wandering around in the wilderness for 40 years because they put their confidence in their own ability rather than in the Lord's. Believe today in his love for you. Know that although there may be challenges ahead the Lord will use them to develop you and grow you. Every obstacle that is put in your path the Lord will use as a stepping stone to take you higher into his purposes and closer to fulfilling the calling He has on your life. He loves you, He is committed to you and He has the best life in store for you, better than anything you could ask or hope for. Trust him and take him at his word today. Begin to live fearlessly!

2

Remember the good days!

*"*T*ake twelve stones from here out of the midst of the Jordan, from the very place where the priests' feet stood firmly, and bring them over with you and lay them down in the place where you lodge tonight."*

Joshua 4 v 3

Can you still remember what you learnt in school? Do your school days feel just like yesterday or are they now a dim and distant memory? I know when my son was preparing for exams last year I found it hard to comprehend how there were subjects I had spent so much time studying for and yet now all the facts seem to have disappeared, like they never existed in my brain. And then I realise other things feel like they only happened yesterday. There are times when we hear a song from years ago, step back into a room or smell a meal that we used to have at our grandparents home and it's as if we are transported back to that very moment.

There are some things we are struggling to remember and there are other things we are trying desperately to forget. Our memories are inconsistent and often hard to work out but the Lord obviously knows what an important part they will play in our lives or he would not have instructed us so many times to *remember* or *not to forget.* So why is it so essential for our Christian walk and what impact does the act of remembering have on us? *"And **remember that you were a slave** in the land of Egypt, and the Lord your God brought you out from there by a mighty hand and by an outstretched arm."* Deut 5:15 These words **remember that you were a slave** are repeated 4 more times in Deuteronomy.

The Lord keeps repeating this so that the Israelites would not forget what the Lord had saved them from. On the days where things didn't look like they were going in the right direction they needed to stop and remember who was in control. You see the more we magnify the work of the Lord in our lives the greater the confidence we will have in His ability to rescue and deliver us in the future.

You would think being released from captivity after 400 years and walking free, loaded with the spoils of your oppressor, would not be an easy thing to forget, let alone the parting of the Red sea and seeing your enemies swallowed up by the very waters that were held back for you. And yet God saw the fragility of human nature and their ability to easily become consumed by the moment. Within such a short time the celebrations stopped and gave way to moaning and complaining as the current trials overwhelmed their thinking and clouded their minds and they began to give way to fear. They appeared to have quickly forgotten who was actually responsible for fighting their battles.

So the Lord commanded that memorial stones be set in place. Twelve stones, one representing each tribe. Every family could look back and see how their line had been saved by the Lord. This was a personal intimate reminder for everyone. Not just for that moment in time but for the generations. What they passed down would impact their sons and daughters and would build future hope and expectation to trust and believe in a God who was not limited by the resources or natural laws of this world. A God of the impossible, a God who is outside of our understanding and who longs to show us life from a heavenly perspective. A God who wanted them to be set free from fear and to live courageously.

It is the same Heavenly Father who invites you to trust in him today. To take account of your own life. The journey that he is guiding you on, the times he has rescued you from poor decisions and bad attitudes. The people he has connected you with who have believed in you & encouraged you. The opportunities that have opened up before your eyes. Remember the Lord today. Thank him for his faithfulness & approach your future with an anticipation of what He wants to do in and through you!

3

The Power of your story!

"Then he spoke to the children of Israel, saying: "When your children ask their fathers in time to come, saying, 'What are these stones?' then you shall let your children know, saying, 'Israel crossed over this Jordan on dry land'; for the Lord your God dried up the waters of the Jordan before you until you had crossed over, as the Lord your God did to the Red Sea, which He dried up before us until we had crossed over, that all the peoples of the earth may know the hand of the Lord, that it is mighty, that you may fear the Lord your God forever."*

Joshua 4: 21-24

There are times I feel bombarded with advice about how I should be parenting my children. Everyday we are surrounded by different voices telling us what they should eat, how they should exercise, what they should be studying and what extra -curricular activities will help them reach their full potential. Too often we feel overwhelmed and fear we are not doing enough. Despite all my attempts to do the right thing, I realised in my own life there was something I was failing to share with my children. There were keys that would set them up for future success that I had overlooked.

In today's passage the Lord clearly displays to us one of the most important things we can do to ensure our children see good days ahead of them. It's the power of our story. It's the word of our testimony. The journey that the Lord has led us on in our daily's lives and the breakthroughs we have seen are not just for us to benefit from, they actually serve as a springboard for our children to say " do it again Lord!"

Look at how important this was to the Lord. He gave specific instructions to the children of Israel about the story they would share with their children. He knew the power of testimony. He knew that these miraculous acts that he had performed for the people could be forgotten. When trials and tribulations came He was aware of how man's head can go down and he can find himself wallowing around in the dust thinking that all hope is lost.

The stones were to be set as a visual reminder. They were taken from the very place of deliverance. From the bottom of the Jordan. Where the people themselves had walked to freedom. Each of these people had seen first hand the Lord's mighty power. If we read carefully as well we see how the Lord not only reminds them of the crossing of the Jordan but also the parting of the Red Sea. It's as if he is saying remember all of my incredible works. You see what I have done before, I have shown you that I will do it again. I am faithful. I have rescued you time after time and have stayed true to my word. Believe in me, have confidence in what I say, trust that I will protect you, provide for you, deliver you and bring you into promise.

The work that the Lord has done in our lives is like pure gold and we get to share this with our children. This is treasure that surpasses any earthly knowledge or wisdom. As we tell them about the Lord's hand on our lives and we take time to remember where we have come from and how he has brought us through we will find faith arising within us as we recognise his power at work. Not only this, we will begin to raise a generation that says no to fear. We will create a platform on which our children can stand boldly in faith and believe with a confident expectation that they can and will receive above all they could ask, hope or imagine.

4

Mind Matters

"**S**umming it all up, friends, I'd say you'll do best by filling your minds and meditating on things true, noble, reputable, authentic, compelling, gracious—the best, not the worst; the beautiful, not the ugly; things to praise, not things to curse. Put into practice what you learned from me, what you heard and saw and realized. Do that, and God, who makes everything work together, will work you into his most excellent harmonies."*

Philippians 4: 8-9

What happens when you take the plunge and try out a new hairstyle? You get 9 compliments about it and one unfavourable remark. I can almost guarantee that your mind will be drawn to the criticism and you will find yourself mulling over those words far more than the 9 positive comments that were made.

Our flesh tends to be drawn towards the negative. If we are left to our own devices we will soon find ourselves on a downwards spiral. In fact, we are often our own worst critics, at times dissecting all our actions, remarks and achievements. Thinking about what we should have said, what people probably thought, and where we keep messing up and getting it wrong.

The Lord is so aware of what we can fill our minds with when we don't keep our thoughts fixed on him. The word tells us that Jesus is the light of the world, He comes into our lives as the light of life. He wants to shine into our hearts each day and bring his love into every part of us. When we live without his word illuminating our minds on a daily basis we soon find ourselves becoming overwhelmed by dark thoughts. We become critical of ourselves and others and magnify the bad that we see until it becomes much bigger than it actually is.

That is why the Lord exhorts us to think on good things. Everything about the Lord is good and true and every blessing in your life is a result of his faithfulness to you. In order for us to live a life full of joy and peace it is essential that we fill our minds with heaven's reality. There is no strife in heaven, there is no fear in heaven, there is no anger or jealousy or bitterness. The word tells us that the Lord has more thoughts about us than there is sand on the seashore. What does that tell us? The Lord has countless thoughts about us that are all good. They are in fact beautiful, praiseworthy, the best and never the worst. The Lord is goodness and love; it is impossible for him to act outside of his nature.

So remember today that you have been given this same nature. " I have been crucified with Christ. It is no longer I who live, but Christ who lives in me. And the life I now live in the flesh I live by faith in the Son of God, who loved me and gave himself for me." Galatians 2:20. This life of love can be entered into fully as we learn to speak the language of the kingdom. When we meditate on everything around us that speaks of God, when we focus on the beauty of creation, the awesomeness of the

Lord's work in your life, the uniqueness of your calling and incredible words of confidence and hope that he speaks over you.

You don't need to look to the left or to the right and be distracted by the race others are running or feel that you need to compete to get the Lord's attention. You don't need to wallow when people mistreat you or stay defeated and afraid that life will pass you by. This is not the truth so do not allow your mind to be filled with fear and lies. The truth is that God has an amazing life for you to enjoy each day, one in which he wants your heart to be immersed in his outrageous love for you, so think on these things. Everything that speaks of love and life is the Father sending you a message today telling you, you're precious, you're his beloved and you are of immeasurable value to Him.

5

Do you want to live a carefree life?

"*Don't fret or worry. Instead of worrying, pray. Let petitions and praises shape your worries into prayers, letting God know your concerns. Before you know it, a sense of God's wholeness, everything coming together for good, will come and settle you down. It's wonderful what happens when Christ displaces worry at the centre of your life.*"

Philippians 4: 6-7

I don't know about you but I know that I don't set out each day with a list of things that I would like to worry about. In fact I try to make a conscious decision not to worry but there are many times that I find that before long there are thoughts flying around in my head that are starting to weigh me down and I am imagining the worst case scenario playing out in front of me. Many people struggle with similar negative thoughts and can feel their emotions changing and even physical symptoms such as a tightening in their chest and their heart rate soaring at times leading to panic attacks as these fears build up and overwhelm them!

The world recognises that worry is a problem that is affecting all levels of society and there is much research around it. When we look at the figures it's incredible to see the kinds of things that we worry about; 40% is about future events that do not happen, 30% is about the past which we cannot change, 12% is over needless health worries and 10% petty concerns. There is only 8% of what we worry about that can be classed as legitimate concerns. That means 92% of our worrying is really over useless things that we can not change or will never happen.

So what does the Lord instruct us to do with our worries? He calls us to turn our worries into prayers. He knows that if we can take these thoughts that are troubling us, that are weighing us down and in many cases affecting our health, and bring them to Him we will find that our perspective changes.

Prayer you see is an interchange, it's a dialogue. However it is not an equal exchange where two sides relate and listen and share burdens. When we pray we come to the Lord and let go. We give to him the weights and burdens that are on our shoulders and in exchange we receive his life and grace.

The Lord knows that there will be things in life that concern us but he shows us that we have a choice about the way in which we think on these things. I believe it is impossible to praise God and worry at the same time. When we praise the Lord we magnify him, we make him bigger. We put our eyes off ourselves, our situations, everything of this world that grapples for our attention and we tune into our true identity as children of the King. We exalt who God is, we remind ourselves that He is above it all, that he reigns on high, that He has always been and will always be. We remember that He is our Heavenly Father who will not withhold any good thing from those who walk uprightly. (Psalm 84: 110) And today because of Jesus we are righteous and can come boldly to the throne of grace knowing that the Lord will help us in our time of need.

I know as I practise this, I find the Lord's peace becoming real to me. The peace that lives on the inside of me begins to permeate my thoughts and where there has been darkness and confusion I find light and clarity. Even when I don't have the answers I have a sense of well being because I have given up trying to be in control and surrendered to the one who has actually been holding it all together all along. Today allow Christ to take the centre stage. Recognise every good work that He has done in your life and magnify his love for you! Your worries and fears will disappear effortlessly!

6

What are you focusing on today?

"I lift up my eyes to the hills. From where does my help come?"

Psalm 121:1

W hat we are looking at will affect where we are going in life. We often hear the expression, 'his heads down at the minute", and that normally describes when someone is feeling a bit low. They are lacking a sense of purpose and direction. They are feeling a bit lost or at sea and are discouraged about the trajectory of their life. This happens when we take our eyes off Jesus. That is why we see in this verse the psalmist is telling us that he is choosing to lift his eyes up. He is looking towards the hills. Now naturally for us to look at hills it requires us to adjust our gaze and take our eyes away from the ground, the dust, the path just in front of us and look afar to a place beyond our reach. The hills signify a high place. Many times in the bible we find accounts of people meeting with the Lord on a mountain top. This is not to say that the only place we can draw close to the Lord is a physical location but the hills are symbolic of that place that is out of the way of the daily grind. It is away from the crowds and the normal run of life. It is a quieter place. In this place on high ground we can physically gain a new perspective. We can look down on life and see it in a new way.

In order for us to truly thrive in life we need to constantly remind ourselves that we are in this world but not of this world. We may be surrounded by the hustle and bustle of daily life, we may be engaging everyday in work, school, running a home or leading a business but we are set apart. We are citizens of a heavenly kingdom and we have a king who is intimately concerned with the affairs of our lives and is greatly invested in seeing us become all that He has created us to be. Our lives may at times look ordinary but what He wants to do in and through us is extraordinary. The Lord wants us to start to see from his perspective. He wants us to lift up our eyes. To get a bigger view of what is up ahead. He is calling us to an adventure with him. He is calling us to dream big, He is calling us to step out and believe in those promises that He has put on our hearts.

What is it that holds you back from just taking the Lord at his word and stepping out in faith? It's when we let our gaze slip, it's the moment we stop looking at Jesus and we start looking at ourselves. We see our inadequacies, our weaknesses, our past failures and our disappointments. Fear begins to creep in as we hear the doubting voice in our heads saying : " How can you trust this time is going to be different from the last?" " Can you cope with the disappointment again?" "What will people say if it doesn't work out?" If we entertain any voice other than the voice of the Lord we will become defeated and deflated and our heads will sink back down to the ground and our eyes will become dim and our vision will have faded.

Where does your help come from today? When the psalmist wrote this it was not because he didn't know the answer to the question, rather

17

he was encouraging himself to consider again the goodness of God. To remember again what He had done in his life and to build faith once more for what he will continue to do in the future. He was exhorting himself to live a fearless life and to choose to trust God's word above any situation he may be facing.

7

Where does your help come from?

"My help comes from the Lord, who made heaven and earth. He will not let your foot be moved; he who keeps you will not slumber. Behold, he who keeps Israel will neither slumber nor sleep."

Psalm 121 v 2-4

When my son was studying for his exams I found he would often come to me for help in most of his subjects apart from when it came to maths. This was because he had worked out that his Mum's knowledge of maths was pretty rusty and rather than sit through an hour of YouTube videos while she tried to work out the answer it was better to wait for Dad who could normally figure it out pretty quickly.

Many people in life can offer us help but if they are not qualified for the task it does not bring us much comfort when we are in desperate need. That is why we see the psalmist today reminding himself of who he is coming to. Our help is from God Almighty. Our help comes from the one who created the entire universe. The one who spoke the world into being, the one who gives us our very breath. When we approach him we can have confidence that He will be more than able to come to our aid.

Not only is the Lord qualified to meet our needs and has all the resources of heaven at his fingertips, He is willing! You see we learn from this psalm that Yahweh was not like the other deities that were worshiped in ancient eastern cultures. In those times many Gods were often depicted as sleeping, they were seen as having need for rest just like us mere mortals. But our God is set apart. He keeps us, or watches us. The word in Hebrew that is used here is the word '*Shamar*'. This word does not describe a passive action but rather a God who seeks to guard and protect us. We see this same theme echoed in Psalm 91:4, "*He will cover you with his feathers, and under his wings you will find refuge.*" There is a tender care as a mother bird shields her young so shall the Lord shield you from all danger and harm.

What is more the Lord will ensure that you are firmly established. Whatever ground you have taken He will not allow it be stolen from you. Your feet are anchored on solid ground as He holds you in his love. You do not need to fear, no matter what threats may rise up against you, nothing will be able to creep past the watchful eye of your loving Heavenly Father. He will intervene in your life, He will take care of you, He will preserve you in times of trouble, He will deliver you from evil. He will be your shield, your protector and shelter.

Whatever you are going through today, have confidence that God is by your side, every minute of the day. 24/7 his watchful eye is concerned with every detail of your life. He doesn't stand back from a distance and watch you struggle and stumble your way through life. He is carefully guarding you. He is attentive to your needs, He is all powerful and desires to intervene and will ensure that whatever lies ahead, you do not need to be afraid, he will not let your foot slip.

8

Guard your heart!

"Above all else, guard your heart, for everything you do flows from it."

Proverbs 4:23

A re you someone who is good at following instructions? I have to admit that when it comes to DIY I tend to get a bit impatient if I see pages and pages of detailed steps to follow. This probably explains why some of my "creations" don't always end up looking how they are supposed to! If I had only taken my time and done as was suggested I would have had much better results!

When we find instructions in scripture it is even more important that we take time to understand exactly what is being said. There are too many times when we just pick out a verse but don't seek to understand it in a wider context and then it can fail to have the impact that the Lord intended.

One of the important principles to remember is the law of first mention. So where does the Lord first talk about the heart? *"The Lord saw that* the wickedness of man was great in the earth, and that every intention of the thoughts of his heart was only evil continually" Gen 6:5. When man is left to his own devices the intentions of his heart turn towards evil. The Lord has seen throughout history the devastating effects of man turning from his ways and following his sinful desires. That is why the Lord gives these specific instructions in today's verse. He loves us so much that he doesn't want us to fall into any of the traps of the enemy and reap the consequences of bad decisions in our lives. He desires to see us walking into all that he has promised and living lives where we can reach our full potential so how do we ensure that we can guard or keep our hearts?

In today's verse the Lord is telling us about the importance of guarding our hearts, but in the preceding verses He shows us how to do this. *'My son, be attentive to my words; incline your ear to my sayings. Let them not escape from your sight; keep them within your heart'.* (Proverbs 4:21) In order for us to guard our hearts we need to ensure that we have made the word a priority in our lives. We do this when we purposefully take time to listen to it, when we ponder it, when we keep it at the forefront of our minds. When we fill our thoughts with God's word we will see good results. Not only will we find life- true life, not mere existence but we will actually get to thrive. In fact in verse 22 we see how this will affect every part of us including our physical healing. *'For they are life to those who find them, and healing to all their flesh'* v. 22

You see God's word is powerful. We know from John 1 that Jesus himself is the, *'Word become flesh'*. As we read the word we get to commune with Jesus and his life flows in us and where there is life and love there can be no fear because as 1 John 4:8 tells " perfect love expels all fear. If we are afraid, it is for fear of punishment, and this shows that we have not fully experienced his perfect love." Allow his words of life to sink into your heart and see your fears melt away.

9

Taking from Jesus

"**N**ow if God so clothes the grass of the field, which today is, and tomorrow is thrown into the oven, will He not much more clothe you, O you of little faith?**"

Matthew 6:30

As parents, my husband and I have learnt to work as a team. If I hear the words "... but Daddy says..." my kids have now realised that I will always check that statement out before I act so that I am not duped into one of their schemes to get something they are not supposed to be having. There are times when I can tell instantly that there is no way on earth that Daddy has agreed to that. You see when we know each other well we can attest as to whether the words sound like they come from a person or if they are being misrepresented. I have found in my Christian walk that there have been passages in the Bible that I have read and then struggled to reconcile with what I know about the character of Jesus. Somehow what is written doesn't seem to match up with what I know of Jesus in the word and experience of him when I commune with him each day. It's important that we are mindful that we read translations of the Bible and at times there can be parts that have not been accurately interpreted or we have failed to understand the context in which the passage is set.

This particular passage is one such example. The phrase "O you of little faith" occurs 5 times in the gospels. When I used to read this I believed it was a rebuke from Jesus. I thought that He was frustrated or annoyed with the disciples for not believing in his power to change situations and I concluded that He was tired of dealing with their unbelief. However I realise if I stop for a minute and challenge my thinking my conclusion is not consistent with Jesus' behaviour towards his disciples. He is endlessly patient and does not get easily annoyed. In fact the only anger he ever demonstrates is towards the religious leaders who try to make it difficult for people to draw close to God. It's in these instances that we hear his harsh rebuke. So what does this statement actually mean? Little-faith "*oligópistos*" describes someone dull to hearing the Lord's voice, or disinterested in walking intimately with Him. So what the Lord shows us here is that for every area of your life, do not be dull to see what the Lord can do. What do you see? What do you perceive?

The 5 times we see this phrase we can see that Jesus is reminding us of his grace and care and concern for every detail of our lives. In Matthew 6:30 it says that "if God clothes the grass of the field, how much more will He clothe us?" He shows us that we need not worry about being clothed. He will provide for us! In Matthew 8:26 He rebukes the storm with one word: "Shalom," showing us we need not be afraid of anything. In Matthew 14:31 He pulls Peter up when he is sinking under the waves showing us we can always be assured that He will save us. In Matthew 16:8 He fed 5,000+ people. We need not fear we will lack for anything. Finally, Luke 12:28 He reiterates the clothing of the grass of the field. He again assured us that He will take care of all our daily needs and the concerns of everyday life.

The Bible tells us that we receive everything from God by faith. So, faith means "to take." What Jesus is really saying is "Why do you trust in me so little that you take so little from me? Take more! Take as much as you want!" What a wonderful way to rebuke, telling them they are not taking enough! So when you approach the Lord today, come believing in an extravagant Father who longs to lavish his love, acceptance and grace on his children and see them take every good gift He has for them.

10

The life giving source within!

"I have food to eat of which you do not know."

John 4:32

"What time is tea going to be?" is a regular question in our house. Perhaps even more frustrating is "What are we having for tea?" Particularly at 8am when we have only just finished breakfast. I don't know about you but I feel that the subject of food can easily take a lot of our attention between shopping, preparing, cooking and cleaning up! Food is a central part of everyday life. It's one of our most basic needs and it reminds us of our humanity. We need to take time out, we need to stop and eat, we need to replenish ourselves in order to survive and perform at our best.

Jesus although fully God took on the form of man when he walked on the earth. He would have experienced tiredness, hunger and thirst just like we do. That is why we see the disciples coming to him in John 4 and urging him to eat. They had all gone into the town in Samaria to get food while Jesus had stayed at the well. However, Jesus answers them with a remark that they do not understand. *'I have food to eat of which you do not know'. John 4:32* The disciples thought at first that Jesus was talking about having eaten in their absence and they wondered how that was possible as there were no shops close by. Yet, the food Jesus was talking about was not physical food. You see Jesus was fed when he did the will of the Father. What Jesus was showing them was that there was a deeper hunger that only our Father can satisfy. When we eat physically we are satisfied but quickly need to feed again. But the Lord can feed us in our spirits and that comes not by taking from others but by giving to them.

This often doesn't make sense to our carnal minds. how can we be replenished if we give away? In the natural we become fearful and become anxious about not having enough for ourselves. But following Jesus' example should bring us into greater levels of freedom and we will ultimately live fearless lives.

The fact is that it is God who created us, he made us with a unique design, we are made in his image and when we follow his ways we will find life, peace and joy. You see we are created to be a blessing. We are image bearers and when we operate in keeping with our true nature we will find purpose and walk into our destiny. So many of us are looking to fill the deepest hunger in our hearts and we allow our focus and attention to be on ourselves but when we keep our eyes on the Father and allow the Spirit of Jesus to lead and guide us everyday we will find that he puts many opportunities in our paths to look beyond ourselves and pour his love into those around us. This may require us at times to forfeit some of our immediate physical needs or even endure some inconvenience and disruption to our routines but when we allow for him to step in and shake us out of our comfort zones we will find we have encounters that require us to draw from the living water that is within. In fact this living water is described by Jesus as " a spring of water welling up to eternal life." His Holy Spirit is a life giving source within. Whenever we look to refresh others the word tells us that, "*He who refreshes others will himself be refreshed.*" Proverbs 11:25

It's the way of the upside down kingdom that Jesus brought to this world. When we lose our lives we find them. When we give away we receive greater blessing. Today Jesus wants to open your eyes to new opportunities where you can sow love, hope and peace into the people in your world. You might not even feel like you have that much yourself but remember when you take the little that you have the Lord will multiply it and you will find there is enough for everyone and rather than feeling depleted you will have had your fill.

11

God loves to give to you

"The LORD bless you and keep you."

Numbers 6:24

Most children love to receive presents and they struggle to understand that as parents it is even more fun to give them, but this year we were super blessed by our son. He had worked over the summer and for the first time had his own money available to spend at Christmas. We were truly amazed when he decided that he wanted to buy gifts for his sisters, and they were not small gifts. He actually wanted to be really generous and was willing to spend most of what he had earned to see the excitement on their faces and the joy of them receiving a surprise!

You see we have been created in the image of the Father. We have been designed to reflect his glory and we are vessels of his love. What I realised with my son was that He was experiencing what God life really looked like. A life of love, a life of generosity, a life of choosing others first.

Remember today that the Lord's heart is always towards you. If I could see the delight in my son as he had the opportunity to bless his younger sisters - how much more our heavenly father! He is ministered to when he blesses us. That is what brings him pleasure.

We see throughout Scripture that God loves to bless His people. It is important that we understand the enormous power in the blessings of God that are recorded in the word. When we read the Old Testament, we see how God provided instructions for how his priests were to bless the nation of Israel. Today's verses are taken from the aaronic blessing. For ancient Israel, the Aaronic Blessing expressed the highest state of blessing that the nation would enjoy as they were faithful to God. What I love when I study these words is that the Lord originates the blessing — The blessing itself emphasises that it is the Lord who blesses the people and does for them what they cannot do for themselves.

The application is different for you and me as New Covenant believers. Jesus Christ has already given us all of the things that are asked for in the Aaronic Blessing, and they have been granted on a permanent basis. Our direct experience of these things can fluctuate from time to time but this blessing should be a reminder of what you have in Christ today.

And what is more, God's blessing is not just about providing for our material needs, it's about his abundant favour being released into every area of our lives. It includes our relationships, our health, our prosperity, our emotional wellbeing, our physical safety and much more. Everything that could cause us concern or make us fearful is taken care of by the Lord.

How do we access these blessings that the Lord has made available to us through Jesus' finished work? Just as the Lord created the world through what he spoke forth, his blessing comes into our lives through what He declares over us. Therefore we take hold of the blessings and put our Amen to them. We come into agreement with everything that he declares and we speak it forth and through the creative power of our words we call out everything that the Lord has promised for us with confidence and boldness.

Start your day by reminding yourself what the Lord has promised you in his word and declare that you will see his blessing in every area of your life today!

12

Inside out living

"and keep you"

Numbers 6:24

How much is your outside world affecting your inner world? The problem today is that most of us live from the outside in - Our inner state is dictated to and determined by what is happening on the outside. In these times that is a total nightmare as everyday we are bombarded by negative news in the media. But there is also another more subtle message at play in our lives if we are not careful. Our increasing reliance on social media as a way to connect and interact can try and fill that need for longing and acceptance that should only be found in the Lord. We are a generation, and are raising a generation that is conditioned by LIKES. We are looking for the majority opinion before we make our decisions. If we allow this to consume our thinking the result will be that we stop looking to the word and who Jesus says we are and we allow the fluctuating opinions of others to shape how we see ourselves. It happens everyday without us realising. Are the likes to your posts bringing you happiness? Beware that's shaky ground to build upon.

In today's verse we are reminded of the Lord's hand of protection on our lives and we understand that the word repeatedly reminds us of how he will keep us safe. He will watch over us and He will protect us from danger, disease and everything that could harm us physically. For the words in today's verse have the sense of guarding or watching over someone. It means to preserve. For Israel, this would have had a very practical application as they were surrounded by enemies, and God had promised to protect them as long as they were faithful to Him. For you and me, under grace and in the finished work the protection of the Lord is ours today because Jesus was faithful.

But the Lord 'keeping us' means more than just our physical safety. You see, the Lord understands that we have a deep need to feel psychologically safe. He created us with a need to be loved and accepted. Not only do our bodies need to be protected from danger but our hearts too! How many of us as parents would stand back and allow our kids to suffer verbal abuse from others or games of manipulation or control. We understand that these can be just as damaging as a physical attack.

To understand more fully his heart towards us, consider these tender words from Psalm 91:4, 'He will cover you with his feathers, and under his wings you will find refuge'. The Lord gives us pictures so that we can paint a clear image in our minds that will encourage us when we feel afraid or overwhelmed. No matter what is going on on the outside we can experience his peace and experience his love. Today the Lord wants you to know that He will keep you. He will be attentive to every part of your life. He will keep your reputation, when others speak against you. He will guard your mind when negative thoughts attack you, He will surround you with his love and call you beloved when you feel alone.

Don't look for the world's acceptance which will focus on what you do and how you look.

Remind yourself today that you are chosen and accepted by the King of all kings. He will protect your heart, He will bring you the security that you need. You belong to him and because of that you matter and your life is of great significance!

13

He will never turn away from you!

"the LORD make his face shine on you and be gracious to you."

Numbers 6:25

For my husband his favourite part of the day is when he comes home from work in the evening and is greeted by the happy smiley faces of our two girls. They often almost knock him over as he walks through the door and jump up at him wanting hugs and kisses. Then they fight to tell him the latest news of what exciting events have happened at home or probably more likely what mischievous deeds the dog has got up to! It's such a highlight in his day and when he sees them his face lights up.

Have you ever stopped to consider that if we can feel such delight towards being with our kids how much more does our Heavenly Father delight in us!

In today's verse we read about God's face. The theme of the "face" of God has the idea of His people receiving His full attention. The nations surrounding Israel believed in gods who could be distracted by other things and had to be summoned, awakened, or roused to action. This is the background for Elijah's taunts to the prophets of Baal, (1 Kings 18:27–28.) Many pagan religious rituals were designed to attract the attention of the gods and put them in a proper mood to act on behalf of their worshipers, but this was not the experience for the nation of Israel. When the people were faithful to God, His "face" was toward them with the result that they would have peace. God's "face" radiates divine favour. Ancient Israel could expect The Lord's loving, gracious response to their calls for help.

'**The Lord turn his face toward you and give you peace**'. Another beautiful point we find in this verse is in the words "*turn his face towards you.*" Normally when we are disappointed with someone we turn away from them. Physically and emotionally. We separate ourselves in an attempt to protect ourselves. We withdraw because we are disappointed and we don't want to allow ourselves to be hurt again. However the Lord will never treat us in this way. No matter what we do the Lord never turns from us. Romans 8 reminds us: '*What shall separate us from the love of God'?* There is no thing, no one and no sin that will ever subvert the Lord's favour and love towards us. We have been made completely acceptable through the blood of Jesus. Because of his sacrifice the Father can draw close to us today. He is not looking away from you or your situation. He has not turned His back to you. You are never out of His gaze. He is always looking at you and His heart is burning with love for you.

John Gills exposition says this "Show his face and favour, look cheerfully on his people, declare himself well pleased with them in Christ, and appear as smiling upon them through him, indulging them with visits of love, restoring to them the joys of his salvation, and upholding them with his free Spirit; and so causing them to walk pleasantly and comfortably in the ways of God, expecting eternal life and happiness, as God's free gift through Christ."

14

Give my head peace!

" the LORD turn his face toward you and give you peace. "

Numbers 6:26

W hat does the Lord promise you as He looks at you? We read in today's verse that he promises **Peace**! This is a word to centre you. He is not looking at you in judgement. He does not need your best efforts. The Lord is committed to surrounding every aspect in your life with peace.

In the Old Testament, the Hebrew word for peace is "shalom," and in the New Testament, the Greek word is "eirene." The most basic meaning of shalom is complete or whole. In Joshua 8:31, the people refer back to Moses' commands to create an altar of stone that was whole and without cracks with which to make their peace offerings to YAHWEH. So the word here can refer to a stone that is a perfectly whole shape, with no cracks. It can also mean a completed stone wall that has no gaps and no missing bricks. Shalom refers to something that's complex with lots of pieces that's in a state of completeness and wholeness. It's like Job in

5:24. who says his tents are in a state of shalom because he counted his flock and no animals are missing. This is why shalom can refer to our well-being. When David in 1st Sam 17 when he visited his brothers on the battlefield, he asked about their shalom. The main idea is that life is complex, with lots of moving parts, external circumstances, challenges and relationships. When any of these is out of alignment or missing, your shalom breaks down. Life is no longer whole; there is an opening for fear and worry to creep in, it needs to be restored.

In fact, that's the basic meaning of shalom when you use it as a verb. To bring shalom literally means to make complete or restore. So Solomon in 1 King 9:25. brings shalom to the unfinished temple when he completes it. The same goes for human relationships. In the book of Proverbs, 16:7, to reconcile and heal a broken relationship is to bring shalom. And when rival kingdoms make shalom in the Bible, it doesn't just mean they stop fighting; it also means they start working together for each other's benefit. The prophet Isaiah chapter 9:5-6 looked forward to a future king, a prince of shalom. And his reign would bring shalom with no end – a time when God would make a covenant of shalom with his people and make right all wrongs and heal all that's been broken.

That is your covenant right now. As you are reading this right now the Lord's face is shining on you and He is giving you His Peace. This is peace from the storm that feels like it is about to overwhelm you. Every minute waking or sleeping. Every day. Every area. He is bringing Shalom to you as you take your eyes off the temporal and fix your eyes on His eternal promises. This shalom will enable you to live a fearless life because you know that the Lord is taking care of you and working on your behalf.

A word study in the New King James version for SHALOM says: 'Completeness, wholeness, health, peace, welfare, safety, soundness, tranquility, prosperity, perfectness, fullness, rest, harmony, the absence of agitation or discord'.

Let me finish with the words of Jesus in John 14 v 27 - "*Peace I leave with you; my peace I give to you. Not as the world gives do I give to you. Let not your hearts be troubled, neither let them be afraid*".

15

Putting down roots

"Now Jesus was praying in a certain place, and when he finished, one of his disciples said to him, "Lord, teach us to pray."

Luke 11:1

D o you wake up believing that God is more committed to seeing good success in your life than you are? I know I need to continually remind myself of the fact that the Lord is working in my life at all times independent of my performance or feelings on any particular day. His grace towards me is new every morning and He is faithful to his promises. So if God is always for us what is it that can thwart us at times from entering into the fullness of life that he promises?

It is important that we understand the way in which the Lord works and the process it takes for the word of the Lord to come to pass in our lives. When the Lord is sowing the word for the season to come into your life, picture it like Jesus taught us when he talked about the farmer sowing the seed. There are stages in the growth process which lead to new life. Remember the word is a seed, it takes root, grows in us and bears fruit. There is a time that a seed is sown, later there is a time that a seed is harvested but there is plenty of opportunity in the middle for that process to be interrupted. So what is it that gets in the way? I think one of the biggest battles we will face is DISTRACTIONS. Everyday we are plagued with multiple sources coming at us from all directions. Some are internal, in terms of our thinking, fears, insecurities, and others are external whether its Social Media, people, opinions, schedules all vying for our attention and our heart.

Therefore, if we agree that distraction is one of the primary tactics of the enemy to keep us from God's best life, how do we ensure that the seeds that are sown actually take root? When we look to the life of Jesus we know that we can find help for every situation we face. The fact that Jesus came to the earth and took on the form of a man shows us that He knows what it is like to walk in our shoes. He understands the difficulties and challenges that we face. When it came to distractions he was a man who was constantly bombarded with the needs and demands of others and yet he found a way to stay true to his purpose and calling. So we should take a closer look and see what we learn from how Jesus lived his life. As I was writing this I felt the Lord prompting me to study the disciples, they were physically closer to Jesus than any other people. They saw Him open blind eyes, raise the dead, cast demons and yet its only recorded that they asked Jesus to teach them one thing: Luke 11:1 *'Now Jesus was praying in a certain place, and when he finished, one of his disciples said to him, "Lord, teach us to pray'*.

So why is it that this was the one thing that they wanted to learn about above everything else? I believe that they witnessed first hand what happened to Jesus when He went and spent time alone with his Father. Just take a look, for example, at the time Jesus hears about John the baptist being beheaded. The first thing Jesus does is leaves the crowd and goes away. Jesus was fully human and fully God. He felt all the emotions that we would have felt but He learnt to bring all that emotion, all of his humanity and come humbly before his Father to receive everything that he needed. Many times in my life when I have heard tragic news or have felt hurt and betrayed by others I have wanted to withdraw and but I have turned away from everyone including the Lord, or if I have run to the Lord I have put away all thoughts of continuing in his purposes and calling on my life. I have allowed myself to wallow in my pain or grief, believing I need time for me. Jesus operated differently. He had complete confidence and trust in the Father's ability to sustain him. He didn't allow the voices in the crowd or the work of the enemy to bring fear into his heart and to distract him from the call on his life.

Think about your life today. Where is the enemy trying to divert you from entering into your calling? What obstacles is he trying to put into your path? Take time to be with the Father. Allow him to still your heart and centre you again on your God given purpose and don't let anything pull you away from what the Lord is planting in your life.

16

Hearts shaped by Grace

"But Jesus Himself would often slip away to the wilderness and pray in seclusion."

Luke 5:16

A number of years ago my husband and I were flying back from England, there had been some weather issues and we had been diverted to another airport. We were coming into land and the plane was making its usual descent. I was looking out of the window but could see very little as there was thick fog all around us. Suddenly there was an enormous roaring sound. Everyone was thrown back in their seats and the plane quickly began to soar back up into the air! There were anxious cries from across the cabin and a tangible sense of panic filled the air. Now if you were to have asked people before entering the plane if they had a relationship with the Lord and prayed on a regular basis you might have had a mixed response. But I can almost guarantee that at that moment when we were all confronted with the thought that the plane ride might not be as plane sailing as we thought I believe many cries for help to God were being uttered!!

The truth is many of us as believers can neglect our prayer lives or leave intense prayer to moments of crisis, pain or loss. The Lord is always there for us and will always answer us when we call out to him for help. Psalm 118v 5 assures us, "*In my distress I called to the LORD, and He answered and set me free.*" However when we look at the Life of Jesus I believe there are many things that he wants to teach us about prayer. Let's look at the story in Mark 9. The disciples have tried to deliver a boy from a demon and they have failed. It's not that they didn't know what they were doing, they were actually really experienced, in fact the most experienced deliverance team in the world at that time! They were like the A Team! Yet in this instance they were unable to help the boy. They turn to Jesus, He steps in and delivers him. Now, many people would say, well obviously Jesus could deliver the boy He is God after all. But we need to remember the fact that Jesus was operating from His humanity, He was trusting and putting his faith in the Father to bring heaven to earth.

After the child is delivered the disciples take Jesus aside and ask Him how this happened. They want to be able to do it too!! Jesus tells them (vs 28) this kind only comes out through prayer and fasting. Now what is interesting here is that we do not see Jesus praying or fasting at this point. He simply tells the demon to leave. So why is this his answer? You see, we often pray as a reaction or when we are on the defensive but that always leaves us behind the curve. Jesus did fast for 40 days at the start of His ministry which tells us that He was not fasting for a problem, but for a lifestyle. Jesus often withdrew to pray, not in response to a need but because He desired communion with his Father. Jesus knew that all life and blessings come from the Father and it was from this place of connection that he brought victory.

Today Jesus wants us to cultivate a lifestyle of prayer and fasting. He wants us to know him intimately each day. He wants us to commune with him, to hear his heart, to have him impart his faith into our situations so that we are fully equipped for the trials and challenges that might come our way. He knows how powerful fear can be and how we can feel paralysed by anxiety and worry. Rather than letting ourselves feel overwhelmed by difficult circumstances, He wants us to take an offensive position, in which we proactively build ourselves up in the knowledge of him and allow our hearts and minds to be shaped by his grace. In this place we will have boldness and confidence to face every situation with the perspective of heaven and we will see his life flow and change our challenges to opportunities to grow and advance His kingdom on earth!

17

Listen up!

"Find a quiet, secluded place so you won't be tempted to role-play before God. Just be there as simply and honestly as you can manage. The focus will shift from you to God, and you will begin to sense his grace."

Matthew 6:6 (MSG)

I started my career as a primary school teacher, teaching 4-5 year olds. I quickly learned that young children can get easily distracted and that my biggest challenge was holding their attention! One thing I noticed was that if I could maintain eye contact with them they were usually listening to me but if they looked away for a second I had normally lost them to whatever was happening out of the window. So I decided to start using the phrase " Your ears won't work if your eyes are not looking at me!" One day a parent came up to me quite frustrated by how seriously her son had taken this statement. Apparently he would no longer entertain a conversation with his Mum unless he had her full, undivided attention as his teacher had told him her ears weren't working if he couldn't see her eyes!!

There is an important point behind all of this. Where we focus will de-termine how well we can listen. This is true not just in our relationships with others but also in our relationship with the Lord. He wants us to give him our full attention because he knows that only in that place will we truly start to connect with him and receive the life, peace, joy and freedom He died to bring us. As today's verse tells us, He wants us to step away from all the distractions, all those things crowding in for our attention and to find a quiet place, where our eyes will no longer be tempted to drift from him.

Then when we come before him He wants us to come simply and honestly. What does this look like? Well I believe it means come as you are, not as you'd like to be, not as you think you ought to be, but just as you are. When we do this the Lord can help us because there is no pretence, no mask, no playing games. He wants us to be real with him. The truth is He knows it all anyway! The things we might feel ashamed of, the things that we think will displease him, the times we think we have let him down. He sees it all and He loves us the same. Nothing separates us from his love! He wants us to trust him enough that we can come humbly not relying on our good works but totally dependent on his grace. Whenever we do this the true work can begin, this is where the exchange can take place. In this time of intimacy and humility as we surrender ourselves to his mercy we can let go of all the stuff that is weighing us down.

So what actually happens when we pray. To properly understand it we need to look at what the word means: The word pray, 'proseúxomai' is made up of two words: prós, "towards, exchange", and 'euxomai', "to wish, pray." Literally translated it means to interact with the Lord by switching human wishes (ideas) for His wishes as He imparts faith ("divine persuasion.") Therefore as we pray our heart connects with the Father. We come to the cross and give Jesus our mistakes, our insecurities, our worries, our fears, our pride and our pains. We exchange the weight and the burden, the disappointment and the frustration, the fear and worry and in its place we receive the wholeness, and the shalom of the Father made possible through the death and resurrection of Jesus!

Prayer is a place of deep connection where you receive His grace, His love, His perspective in place of the weight and worry of the world. Come to him with confidence today and be expectant that your burdens will be lifted and replaced with his peace!

18

24/7

"Rejoice always, pray without ceasing, give thanks in all circumstances; for this is the will of God in Christ Jesus for you."

1st Thess 5 v 16-18

When I am faced with something difficult if I don't bring it to Jesus I tend to respond in two ways. I either try to avoid it or I throw myself into it and persevere through gritted teeth. Neither of these reactions are particularly helpful. The first leaves me with a feeling of dread and the task just keeps getting bigger in my mind and the second leaves me feeling exhausted and burnt out! Unfortunately there are verses and themes in the Bible that we can treat in this same way. We either find them too difficult to follow and we ignore them or we put all our effort into trying to succeed in an attempt to keep the Lord happy with our performance. Prayer is one of these subjects and many verses that talk about prayer often leave people feeling condemned and unworthy if they don't understand their true meaning.

Let's look at today's verse. On the surface it feels like the person that wrote this must be living some kind of fairy tale life that is not in touch with our reality. Paul is telling us to rejoice at all times, to pray at all times and to give thanks at all times!! Is he just not in touch with real life!! Actually we need to take a step back and remember where Paul was writing from. He wasn't penning these words in his luxury five star hotel overlooking the sea. He was in a prison cell. We also know that Paul was a man who understood God's grace in his life. He didn't say things to impress God or because he felt he needed to do the right thing. His relationship with the Lord was honest and authentic so when he was encouraging other believers to rejoice, pray and be thankful at all times it was because this was the secret to his own walk with the Lord.

"Rejoice always", - How do you do that when things are tough? Outside of Jesus, the only time that you can rejoice is when you are feeling joy. The Lord has a different way for us. So what does the verse actually mean in the original Greek, *'xaírō'* from the root *xar-*, is to be *favorably disposed, leaning towards* and connect with. Then, *'xáris'*, means grace or to properly delight in God's *grace* to rejoice. Literally it means to experience *God's grace (favor)*,and be conscious (glad) for His *grace*. When you do not prioritise His presence where you just connect you are less conscious of His grace. In your life there are only 2 options - you are either leaning towards and delighting in His grace, or you are relying on yourself and what you think you can do.

He then says *"pray unceasingly."*He is encouraging us to connect and exchange our burdens for his grace. Why is this? I think this is about heart health. Proverbs 4:23 *says, 'Keep your heart with all diligence; for out of it are the issues of life.'* Managing your heart is critical for how you experience life because everything flows from there. Keeping your heart in touch with God's heart will mean that His life will flow through you. If you are neglecting this in your life then you will see a lack of life flowing through you.

Finally he tells us to 'Give thanks always," '*euxaristéō*', (eú, "good" andxaris, "grace") – properly, acknowledging that "God's grace works well," i.e. for our eternal gain and His glory; to give thanks – literally, "thankful for God's good grace." Always speak - Jesus your unmerited favour in my life works well! This is the word that Jesus used before He fed the 5,000 with a packed lunch. In those times of exchange and connection in declaring God's grace is enough, what we see is that we have been supernaturally blessed and multiplied so that there is an abundance over and above what is needed.

I heard a psychologist speaking and they said that 90% of issues with mental health are rooted in or traced back to trying to avoid pain. Sometimes we are not that different as believers. We operate by trying to get over things from our past, and navigate challenges trying to avoid pain because we are afraid it will simply overwhelm us. But there is a better way, we can adopt a lifestyle of prayer, of constant communion with the Lord where in those moments of distractions we are no longer overcome but rather we turn to the Lord, lean into his grace and exchange the worry and fear for His life and peace.

19

Having Faith to Believe!

"Therefore I say to you, whatever things you ask when you pray, believe that you receive them, and you will have them."

Mark 11: 2

"I'll believe it when I see it!" That's probably a phrase you've heard before or you might have found yourself saying it at times. It's normally when we have doubts concerning someone's words actually matching up to their actions! We don't have confidence in what they have said due to their past record or our past experience! When it comes to Jesus, however, we should not have these same struggles. There is a complete consistency when it comes to the words Jesus speaks and the things that come to pass. Jesus is reliable 100% of the time. He never exaggerates or manipulates a situation to make things appear to be so. If he says it he will do it. We should have great confidence today when we read these words that Jesus spoke to his disciples. And yet for most of us we do struggle with them as we have had experiences that seem to contradict what Jesus is telling us. Our lives tend to be dominated by our senses, we are trained to respond primarily to what we can see / taste

/ hear/ touch and we see this as being "REAL." So when we pray and things appear not to change, what is going on? Or maybe the question we are asking is at what point does God release his power – when you see it manifest or before that?

The story of Jesus and the fig tree helps us with this. In Mark 11 after Jesus had explained these things about prayer to his disciples he came across the fig tree. When he sees that it is not fruitful he curses it. Now the question we need to consider is this: At what point did the tree die? Was it instantaneous? You see, Matthew's account of this story says that the tree died immediately. *"Immediately the tree withered."*(Matthew 21:19) , but Mark's account explains it in more depth telling us *"In the morning, as they went along, they saw the fig tree withered from the roots."* So what can we conclude from this? Are the 2 accounts a contradiction?

NO! What Jesus demonstrates here is that when He spoke to the tree, it died immediately, but from the roots up! It took 12 hours for the manifestation of that to be seen by the disciples but it died whenever Jesus spoke to it and cursed it. This helps us to understand what vs 24 means more clearly : Believe now and you will see. It may be in 1 sec / 1 min/ 1 day or 1 year. The principle is that we are to believe that we receive from God when we pray. Without any hindrance it will happen straight away but we need to recognise that the manifestation of it might not be apparent immediately to our eyes. When God moves, He moves in the spirit, that is the new creation part of you, perfect and complete! The Spiritual world is as real as the natural world. In fact it is the parent force. But because we are so driven by our senses and everything that we encounter in the carnal, temporal realm, we need to train ourselves to be mindful of the fact that we are living in two realities and the Spiritual realm is the greater force.

Some people approach this with the attitude which says: "I act like it is so when it is not so, in the hope that it will become so." This is not what the Lord is asking us to do, it is not about pretending! So why did Jesus say believe when you pray? Why is that so important? Faith in what God has done is key here. It is a bridge between seeing what God has done in the spiritual realm being manifest in the physical! Hebrew 11 vs 1, *'Now faith is the substance of things hoped for, the evidence of things not seen.'* The word "faith" here is 'PISTIS', it is a firm persuasion, assurance and conviction, "substance" is "hypostasis" a substructure or foundation, and "the evidence of things not seen" is "elehogos' meaning proof or that by which a thing is proved.

FAITH therefore is a conviction of truth that will prove what is not seen acting as a bridge between the natural and supernatural! Today allow what you know of the consistency and the character of Jesus to bring you the assurance and firm persuasion that whatever you have asked of him he will give to you! Shake off the negative thoughts that feed on what your natural senses are telling you and choose to live confidently and fearlessly today!

20

The Lord will never give up on you!

"**T**hen God blessed them, and God said to them, "Be fruitful and multiply; fill the earth and subdue it; have dominion over the fish of the sea, over the birds of the air, and over every living thing that moves on the earth.**"

Genesis 1 v 28

There is something so beautiful and precious about when a child is born and you get to see the delight and joy in the face of its new parents. They marvel at every new sound and movement their baby makes. I can remember when the first baby entered our family and we all sat around watching my little niece, the proud parents, grandparents, aunts and uncles. The TV and normal conversation were replaced by watching this little one sleeping peacefully. At this point all we see is potential, all we think of are the possibilities ahead, all we imagine are the good days the Lord has in store. We are not contemplating the teething stage, the terrible twos, the worry over how they are doing at school, the harsh remarks of supposed friends or the arguing over nights out. We see the beauty of the moment!

Have you ever stopped to think for a moment about how the Lord felt towards Adam and Eve the moment he created them and placed them on the earth? All the thoughts he had had about them, all the times he had dreamt about them, all the things that he had planned. The attention that he had given to the incredible world he had created for them to enjoy. Everything was done for their benefit. The Lord had lavished his love on them. Adam and Eve, our first parents, were to live as priest-kings on God's behalf, replicating and ruling over the world and representing his righteousness to all. They were destined to enjoy the blessings of eternal connection with God. There was only one thing the Lord required of them, one stipulation that he put in place to ensure that their love back to him was a choice. Everything was given to them provided that they didn't eat from the tree of the knowledge of good and evil. To do so, however, would bring the curse of death on humanity.

Unfortunately Adam and Eve chose to disbelieve God and trust their own instincts about right and wrong. They sinned against God, fracturing the human-divine relationship, and plunged us into sin and death. This "*fall*" accounts for the brokenness and corruption we experience in the world today. You and I are living in the results of that - it is in the world all around us but it wasn't the Lord's intention or design that it would be like that for us.

What Adam & Eve demonstrated was that as people we can never live up to our side of the bargain. We will always fall short. Despite our best intentions or our best efforts we can never perfectly keep to our word. There will always be an area in which we fall short and miss it. The problem is we can not deal with the consequences of our rebellion. We choose to disobey or not trust in the Lord's way and yet going it alone brings destruction and pain into our world. Just like Adam and Eve were built to commune with the Lord and live from that relationship, we too live with the innate need for security, for health, for wholeness and to be complete. Everything that the Lord promises in **SHALOM PEACE** are the intrinsic needs that we have as people. But what incredible **HOPE** we have when we look at how the story unfolds, despite man's rebellion the Lord never gave up on his creation. Throughout scripture the Lord has been making covenants with his people through Noah, Abraham, Moses and David all leading to the final fulfillment in Jesus, who ushered in the New covenant of grace. So what does that tell you today?

God is in the business of stepping into man's mess and rescuing him from himself!

Today every obstacle has been removed that could hinder you from receiving the Lord's blessing. No matter how far you might think you have drifted or how dire you might think your situation is, the Lord has gone ahead of you and made a way for you to receive his love and grace. Do not live in fear today thinking you have stepped outside of his love. He has dealt with your sin and your rebellion, he is not surprised by your pride or your stubbornness. He has been dealing with it from the beginning of creation. He doesn't give up on you or lower his expectations of what He has ordained for you. He has Shalom peace for you to enjoy everyday of your life.

21

See things from God's perspective

"*This man shall not be your heir; your very own son shall be your heir.*" *And he brought him outside and said, "Look toward heaven, and number the stars, if you are able to number them."* *Then he said to him, "So shall your offspring be." And he believed the Lord, and he counted it to him as righteousness.*"

Genesis 15 v 3

Do you know that God wants to continually fill your mind with great pictures about your future? At times when you struggle to see what good could be coming up ahead he is encouraging you to imagine a life without limits! He wants you to lift your eyes from the physical, natural realm, with all that is tangible, and he calls you to enter into His realm of the spirit where life itself is formed and spoken into being.

You are probably familiar with the story of Abraham. He had received an incredible promise from the Lord concerning his future, his destiny and his legacy. *"I will make you into a great nation and I will bless you; I will make your name great, and you will be a blessing! Genesis 12* . What a word!

How awesome to receive such a great prophecy over your life! And yet we see how Abraham wrestles with this as circumstances fail to line up with what he had heard. Do you have these same difficulties? Are there times when you believe you have heard from the Lord only to find that your reality is not matching up with the picture you believe the Lord has given you?

By chapter 15 as time has moved on and everything stays the same we see Abraham creating his own version of his destiny : *Lord you have given me no children so a servant must be my heir.* Abraham doubts again that the Lord's promise will come true so the Lord decides to give him a picture to meditate on. He tells him to count the stars. Now, there are two interpretations of this passage. The first is the most obvious, literally count the stars! One by one! I don't know if you have ever tried it but it is an impossible task, which is precisely why the Lord instructs him in this way. He is making it clear that He would bless him with a family that would be beyond anything he could imagine.

A second interpretation of this verse believes this was not the Lord simply saying look how vast the stars are but, recount the story of the stars. See how they depict the gospel. In Bible times the Hebrew word for the 12 Zodiac constellations was called the " Mazzaroth", as mentioned in Job 38: 31-32. So when Abraham went out at night and looked at the sky what could he see? Virgo, the virgin through whom the Messiah would come, Libra a pair of scales, the picture of justice and righteousness, below the scales is a cluster of stars which form the picture of a slain animal, representing Jesus, the lamb of God. Next to the lamb is the cluster of stars called the Southern cross. The scales of justice are balanced through Jesus on the cross. Then we find Scorpio, the man holding a snake and stepping on a scorpion and at the end of the constellation we find Leo, Jesus himself " The Lion of Judah" who reigns forever! When

Abraham looked at the stars they pointed to how a saviour would come and deliver the people and how through Abrahams' seed all the nations of the earth would be blessed.

The Lord took what Abraham looked at everyday and got him to see it differently. The world that is before his eyes suddenly takes on new meaning as the Lord unveils his purpose and gives Abraham a new picture to meditate on. How many times is the Lord calling us to see situations and circumstances from a different perspective? How many times do we think nothing is happening or our minds can only see roadblocks and yet the Lord wants to show you beauty, destiny and purpose in it all. Do you need to lift your head up today? Ask the Lord to show you things from his vantage point and discover all that He has in store for you? Believe that you can live a life of destiny and step out fearlessly!

22

Nothing can stop God's plans for his people

"*On the same day the Lord made a covenant with Abram, saying: "To your descendants I have given this land, from the river of Egypt to the great river, the River Euphrates."*"

Genesis 15 v 18

Do you tend to find there are some words in the bible that you skim over without stopping to appreciate their true significance? I must admit the idea of covenant is one of those. It's something I have a limited understanding of and yet it is such an integral part of how the Lord relates to his people and it shows us a further dimension of his love and grace towards us. So what is a Covenant?

Well, a covenant is a chosen relationship or partnership in which two parties make binding promises to each other and work together to reach a common goal. They're often accompanied by oaths, signs, and ceremonies. Covenants contain defined obligations and commitments, but differ from a contract in that they are relational and personal. Think of marriage. In love, a husband and wife choose to enter into a formal relationship binding themselves to one another in lifelong faithfulness and devotion. They then work as partners to reach a common goal, like building a career or raising children together. That's a covenant. This type of relationship is very common in the Bible. There were personal covenants between two individuals (think David and Jonathan in 1 Samuel 23) and political covenants between two kings or nations (again, think King Solomon and King Hiram in 1 Kings 5 ,

Covenanting was part and parcel of what it meant to live in the ancient eastern world. It makes sense then that God would reach out to us humans to reveal himself and bring about reconciliation through a structure they already understood. So what did He do? The first step God takes in repairing this partnership is to select a small group of people and make a new partnership with them called a "covenant." In this covenant, God makes promises to these people and asks them to fulfil certain commitments. In total, there are four Old Testament covenants—one with Noah, (I will no longer destroy the earth) one with Abraham, (you will be blessed and your descendants will fill the earth and through them I will build my family) one with the Israelites (the law, you do and I will do for you) and one with King David (the messiah would come through your line.) All these covenants serve the purpose of creating a new partnership into which God can eventually invite you and me to be a part of. Unfortunately, Israel eventually breaks these covenants with God.

Nevertheless, throughout the Old Testament, prophets talked about a day when God would once again create a new covenant, one that would completely restore all the broken covenants that came before it. This fifth and new covenant was fulfilled through Jesus. And moreover we see how all the other covenants were fulfilled in him. Jesus is a descendant of Abraham, allowing him to fulfil the covenant God had with Abraham and his family. We're also told that Jesus is the faithful Israelite who is able to truly obey the law, and he is the king from the line of David. Therefore restoring all the covenants in the Bible that God had made with his people!

What I see in all of this is no amount of human weakness or error can thwart the plan of God for his people. Despite our unfaithfulness he remains true to his word. Despite our dysfunction and inability to choose the right way He has worked through the generations, bringing his covenant people to a place where they are finally freed from all their mistakes, fears and doubts and able to enter into a life of blessing. Now we get to live in the richness of the new covenant. Not one where we have to keep our part of the bargain to be able to receive his goodness but one in which Jesus kept it for us!

23

He understands your doubts and assures you with a promise.

" **H**e said to him, *"Bring me a heifer three years old, a female goat three years old, a ram three years old, a turtledove, and a young pigeon."* *And he brought him all these, cut them in half, and laid each half over against the other. But he did not cut the birds in half...* ....*When the sun had gone down and it was dark, behold, a smoking fire pot and a flaming torch passed between these pieces. On that day the Lord made a covenant with Abram,"*

Genesis 15 v 9

Are there times when you find your faith wavering? You know about the goodness of the Lord, you have heard testimonies of his provision and you have even seen it manifest in your own life and yet there are still nagging thoughts at the back of your mind that just won't go away. Can I keep expecting to see good days? Others have experienced pain and loss, someone you know is fighting a life threatening disease, some else has just lost their job. At times we can be surrounded by difficult situations or we can be facing trials of our own. If we're not careful and we allow ourselves to dwell on these difficult circumstances without letting the Lord's light shine into them, we will find that fear begins to creep into our hearts. This results in us starting to question and doubt whether the Lord will prove himself to be faithful one more time.

Abram was struggling with these same doubts. Although the Lord had given him a promise he still hadn't seen it come to pass and he was starting to try and come up with his own solutions concerning the future. Firstly, the Lord assures him that he will have a son of his own. Next the Lord addresses his concerns over the land that he will inherit. In order to assure Abram of his commitment to him the Lord decides to make a covenant.

This would have been a very normal part of life in the ancient Eastern world. So the Lord chose to communicate to Abram in a language that He understood plain and simply. It's as if he was saying " Let's sign a contract and settle this once and for all."Now most of us understand that a contract is an agreement between two parties where each of them commit to upholding their side of the deal. A covenant sealed in blood serves to show the serious nature of the agreement. The parties are saying "If I break this covenant , let this same bloodshed be poured out on me!"

What is special about this covenant is the part Abram plays. He kills and cuts the animals into two and waits to meet with the Lord so that as the custom dictates they will both pass between the pieces to seal the agreement. However we read that the Lord did not appear straight away as Abram had to drive away vultures from eating the flesh. Next we find Abram has fallen into a deep sleep and as he dreams the Lord shows him what the future holds. While Abram sleeps, a smoking pot and flaming torch appear and pass between the pieces. The smoking pot speaks of how the Lord reveals himself as a cloud in the wilderness and later on Mount Sinai, The torch reminds us of how the Lord revealed himself as the burning bush or the pillar of fire in the wilderness. The Lord is showing us that Abraham never signed the contract. As he slept the Lord went through. Therefore Abram could never break a contract that he had not even signed. God alone established the terms and then took on the responsibility of keeping them.

Today we can have this same assurance about our inheritance. We enter into the new covenant by faith in Jesus. We receive everything from the Lord, not by our works or effort but through the sacrifice of Jesus. The Lord ensured that there would be nothing that we could do that could eliminate us from walking into life eternal with our loving heavenly Father.

24

Approach the Father with confidence today!

" And He took bread, gave thanks and broke it, and gave it to them, saying, "This is My body which is given for you; do this in remembrance of Me. Likewise He also took the cup after supper, saying, "This cup is the new covenant in My blood, which is shed for you."

Luke 22: 19-20

Do you try your best to be a person of your word? I'm sure most of us do but as imperfect people we know that despite our best efforts there are many times we fail to deliver everything we have promised. We have many great intentions and want to believe that we will be able to fulfill all of our commitments but there are times when we end up disappointing people or letting them down as we just haven't managed to keep to our side of the bargain. It might be our spouse, our kids, friends, colleagues or people in church, it doesn't really matter who, but what is great for us to know today is that even when we disappoint each other, the Lord never changes how he feels about us.

When Jesus announced this new Covenant He was talking about a new type of relationship that we could enjoy with the Father. If you know much about covenants you will know that they require two parties to make an agreement, or promise that each side swears to keep. In yesterday's verses we saw how God made a covenant with Abraham. But God in his mercy spares Abraham the consequences of human failure by putting Abraham into a deep sleep and taking on the responsibility himself to fulfill the covenant.

Today we see as Jesus introduces this new covenant He breaks the bread in two. Here he points back to the ceremony performed centuries earlier and he shows once more that the two sides of the covenant will be fully realised through his death and resurrection. Abraham was required to kill the animals and cut them in two to signify the two parts of the covenant. Here as Jesus breaks the bread in two he is reminding people of the former covenant and showing them that once more the Lord is providing a way for his people to receive the fullness of his grace. This is a permanent solution that will no longer require man to look to his own ability and effort. What's more the Lord is saving you and me from the horrible consequences of our failure. Just as in the covenant with Abraham the smoking pot and flaming torch passed between the pieces. Jesus, as he breaks the bread and offers it with the wine, demonstrates that He will pass through and suffer on our behalf. His body will be torn apart and his blood will be shed at the cross, paying the price that was necessary for us to be able to receive the unconditional love of the Father.

Can I say that this act of supreme love and generosity gives us faith today. He is the faithful one who is precisely faithful in the very areas that we are unfaithful. He knows that you and I will fail but He has already provided for that because He chose to go through for us. So each time we fail and feel condemned, whenever we are sick, worried or we need hope and strength we can approach the Father with complete assurance knowing that through the work at the cross Jesus passed through death and has made the way for us to receive life.

25

Are you seeing His victorious life flowing in you?

"**God chose things the world considers foolish in order to shame those who think they are wise. And he chose things that are powerless to shame those who are powerful'.**

1 Corinthians 1:27

There are times when I find myself getting tied up in knots when it comes to operating in the power of the Spirit. Although I am aware of the Lord's goodness and grace and I understand what the Lord has provided for me, there are times I can find myself falling into negative thinking and I feel myself dwelling on unhelpful thoughts. I let doubt and fear creep in. I get frustrated with myself because it is always the same types of things that I trip up on, my insecurities, questions around my identity, significance. What I realise is the enemy always wants to keep us locked in the same prison cells, playing the same stories over and over in our minds. What have I done? Why can't I be like...? What is wrong with me? I think one of his greatest weapons is to get our eyes off what we do have and onto where we think we are lacking. This got me thinking about how important it is to recognise and use what the Lord has given us. What has he placed in our hands?

You see Jesus describes his Spirit in John 4 as living water. He talks about how out of our innermost being this living water will flow. Now we all know that for water to flow it requires movement, it means it has direction, it moves from one place to another. I believe one of the keys to finding ourselves experiencing more of Jesus in our lives will be when we start to prioritise the things that are important to Him and we allow his heart to shape our directions and goals. It's time to activate what's within - trust in his work- and expect results! This life is not supposed to be complicated! The Lord has made it simple! We just need to simply believe!

So the challenge for me and you today is to step out and believe in what the Lord has done for us! Give away what He has done. Share it with others, speak his word, demonstrate his grace, pray with authority and believe that you will see results. As God's people we know that we are not called to just survive but to thrive. Whatever is going on in us if we draw from Jesus our source we will have grace to pour love into those around us. When we choose to be thankful and focus on his goodness we can start right now and share what the Lord has done in us. The stories so far, his faithfulness, his protection, his healing and his provision.

For many people it just feels too offensive to believe that we can prosper and see good success in life when we simply put our trust in someone else. But that is precisely what the Lord is calling us to do. What seems foolish to man is the wisdom of God. We receive not because we are worthy but because He is! We can step out in faith not because we are faithful but because He is. Put your confidence today in what Jesus has done and what He can do through you. He wants you to be ready, to be open and to be bold. To simply believe. To start to recognise the power he has placed on the inside of us and the life that we can experience flowing through us and impacting others all around with fullness, hope and peace.

26

Do people see you as ordinary?

" **O**ne day Peter and John were going up to the temple at the time
of prayer—at three in the afternoon. Now a man who was lame
from birth was being carried to the temple gate called Beautiful,
where he was put every day to beg from those going into the temple courts. "

Acts 3: 1-2

Have you encountered times of trial or tragedy in your life? I know
for most of us there will be times that we look back on where we have
experienced pain and loss, but for the large part these are seasons we
walk through. In today's verse we meet someone who has only known
hardship, a man totally dependent on others to function in life. Everyday
he has to beg, calling out to people as they pass by on their way to the
temple. We don't know much about his past, but what we do know is that
he was lame from birth. In anyone's estimation this has not been an easy
life. Especially in a culture where disability or sickness was often seen
as being a result of your own sin! This hardly bred a culture of empathy
and compassion.

When He sees Peter and John we are told that he calls out to them and asks them for money. This made me think. He treated them as ordinary, he treated them as everyday people. He treated them in the same way that he would treat any other person. But the fact was they weren't ordinary. They had been commissioned by the Messiah, they had received power from on high, they were living by faith in Jesus and his finished work.

How many people are treating you and me as ordinary today? How many people can we surprise with words of life or prayer that could turn their world upside down? Peter and John did not have what the man was looking for but they did have what he needed.

Imagine they had given him financial aid that day. What would have changed for the man? Well he could have had enough money to buy food, but he would have still had to rely on others to go and get it. Even if they had supplied enough to mean that he would never have to beg again, he would still have been subject to a life of dependency on others to do even the simplest of tasks. Money was the only thing the man could see that would help him out of his predicament. If people have never encountered Jesus they can not really understand what they are missing out on. They will look for what they believe will bring them happiness, or joy or will temporarily help their problem. But with Jesus it is never a temporary fix. He will always go to the root of the issue.

I love how every detail that the bible records serves to bring deeper insight. We are told that this miracle takes place at 3pm. This man's legs are restored to strength at the time of the afternoon sacrifice. Now if we rewind a number of weeks earlier it would have been the precise time when Jesus cried out " *It is finished*", and drew his last breath. Here the Jews are still carrying out their sacrifices in the temple each day atoning for their sins and yet Jesus has already paid the price and now his followers are about to demonstrate the freedom and life that results from living a life of faith in the finished work of the cross!

So whatever you find yourself doing today, remind yourself of who you are in Christ. You are not ordinary. You are not limited by the natural systems of this world. You have a supernatural God living on the inside of you who can set the world on its head and turn lives around. Be open to the Spirit's leading and believe in his power in you today.

27

Simply Believe!

"When he saw Peter and John about to enter, he asked them for money. Peter looked straight at him, as did John. Then Peter said, "Look at us!" So the man gave them his attention, expecting to get something from them. Then Peter said, "Silver or gold I do not have, but what I do have I give you. In the name of Jesus Christ of Nazareth, walk."

Acts 3: 3-6

How much time do we spend focusing on what we don't have? How many times do we talk ourselves out of helping someone because we believe we don't have the time, or the resources or the expertise? Most beggars will be used to being passed by. In fact many people even today have problems looking a beggar in the eye. Normally they are suspicious or fearful or feel embarrassed at their lack of ability to help or change their suffering.

This is not how Peter and John respond. They look straight at him. In fact the word says they looked intently. They gave him their full attention.

You see the man sat in that same place every day and the disciples went to pray at the temple everyday, so the chances are they would have passed each other many times, and the man could have called out many times. But there is something about this particular time that gets their attention.

I believe this is the prompting of the Holy Spirit. I believe the disciples had that inner knowing. Through a lifestyle of prayer and devotion to following Jesus and being empowered through the Holy Spirit, their ears are in tune to that inner voice and their eyes see beyond what is just going on around them and see they how they can bring heaven to earth.

Peter turns to the man and says *"Look at us!"* He asks for his full attention. The word used is blepo, meaning a deep or spiritual insight. In other words it's as if he was saying " you see us, but really look at us!" *"So the man gave them his attention, expecting to get something from them."* Now we see from the beggar's response that he is expectant. Rather than being overlooked someone has responded to his cry for help. Hope rises in his heart. Maybe these men will show him kindness. The man is ready to receive. He believes that he will be shown favour.

What I love about the next part of the passage is the simple, straightforward, uncomplicated statement of faith from Peter. *"Silver or gold I do not have, but what I do have I give you."* These men had nothing to offer the beggar in the natural, but I love the fact that they don't even stop to consider their lack. They don't deny it but it doesn't limit them in any way. They have a revelation of what they do have. They have experienced the abundance of the kingdom. They simply believe that the life of Jesus that they have living on the inside of them can flow into this man and change his life. They can reach out, lift this man out of his suffering, his shame, his limitations and his lowly existence and they can lift him up to receive life. True life, the life of Jesus. So they simply command "*In the name of Jesus Christ of Nazareth, walk.*"

Peter and John simply believed and put their faith in Jesus. They didn't stop and question if they were qualified. They didn't ask the man if he believed. They didn't take time to think about what the people would think and they didn't worry about whether they would upset the religious authorities. They didn't think about whether they were worthy and if any sin on their part would stop the power of Jesus flowing through them. They acted boldly, they acted fearlessly and they acted with confidence not in themselves but in their saviour. They simply believed!!

28

See people raised to life again!

"*T*aking him by the right hand, he helped him up, and instantly the man's feet and ankles became strong. He jumped to his feet and began to walk.*"*

Acts 3:7

There are times in life when we all need a hand. When we need someone to help us out of a situation that has overwhelmed us or a problem to which we can't seem to find a way out of. That is why the Lord has not left us alone. He has put us in community, he has given us a family. A place where we can find help, support, love and encouragement. You see the body of Christ is the Lord's master plan to make sure that we can enjoy the fulness of life that he died to bring us and to see other people finding this freedom, joy and purpose.

This is what I love about today's verse. It's like a master class in how the body of Christ should function. Firstly, we see how Peter responds to the prompting of the Holy Spirit. He sees this man, speaks healing over him and then he helps him up. Peter's actions prove that he had faith that his words carried power. He didn't just speak and then look at the man expecting him to jump up on his own. He demonstrated to the man that this Jesus he spoke of will change your life and he reached out to him encouraging him to believe in this awesome power. What I believe happens here is that the man and Peter join together, they come into agreement with what has been declared. They believe the words and act upon them and it is in this moment that the man gained his strength. As Peter stretched out his hands and helped him up we read that the man's ankles and feet became strong.

Secondly, look at the details that are included here. Peter takes him by the right hand: In bible times the right hand was used to greet a friend or someone at your station in life. When Peter reached out his right hand he was treating the lame man as an equal. Peter was reaching out his hand to a man who had spent his life time on the ground, begging for a living, being literally looked down on by everyone. Now the man is restored by the Lord and Peter lifts him up.

Finally, we find another incredible truth when we study the word here used to describe how Peter helps him or lifts him up. The word is 'egeiro', which is literally raised him up. In fact it can also be used to describe resurrection, literally bringing someone back to life. Look at it in this context. Peter is showing this man the resurrection power of Jesus, bringing him out of death into a new life. He is restored physically but he has also encountered the power of the living God and the life of Jesus and he will never be the same again.

What a picture of our amazing role as the church today. We are equipped to go out and speak life to people who don't know Jesus but who are calling out for help. We can show them his incredible power and help them out of their troubles. We can raise them up as they step out of darkness and receive God's love and grace and we can show them the right hand of friendship and treat them with the dignity, respect and worth with which Jesus sees them. Let's have eyes to see who Jesus is leading us to today and let's dare to believe that we can be used to see lives touched and transformed by his grace.

29

Share your joy and see lives transformed!

"**T**hen he went with them into the temple courts, walking and jumping, and praising God. When all the people saw him walking and praising God, they recognized him as the same man who used to sit begging at the temple gate called Beautiful, and they were filled with wonder and amazement at what had happened to him."

Acts 3:8-10

When you have an encounter with Jesus your life will never be the same again! It will change the company you keep, how you use what God has given you and it will turn you into a person of praise! This is precisely what happens in the next part of the story as we see how the lame beggar responds to the power of Jesus in his life. One of the most important things to note is that he followed the disciples. Once he was healed and restored his number one choice was to be with the disciples and for the first time he was able to come into the temple. He is no longer left at the gate, on the outside, watching life pass him by. He can now be part of the new community of faith.

Secondly, look at what he is doing. He is walking and leaping. He is recognising how he has been restored and he is taking full advantage of this new life he can now experience. Notice he isn't hobbling along, or stumbling. The Lord has fully restored this man and he is making sure everyone can see. The man everyone was used to seeing sitting stuck in one spot was now leaping around!! And finally what reaction did this result in? He praised God! He knew above anything else that there was no other explanation for his healing. He had had an encounter with Jesus. His life had been completely transformed and it will never be the same again.

This is what will happen in our lives when we say: 'what I do have I give to you.' We will see people who have been living on the outside, on the edge of church, feeling like an outsider in life, living on the fringes, not belonging. These people will suddenly want to join you, they will find a place in a loving community where they will have their dignity restored, where the right hand of friendship will be offered to them, where they will be treated as an equal.

When you say: "What I do have I give to you ...," you will find people lifted out of their brokenness and despair and suddenly embracing the gifts that God has given them, finding freedom in life and being healed of their pains both physically and emotionally. And more than this people will turn to the Lord. They will praise God and they will enter into a life of praise and giving thanks as they see what they have been saved from and what life they now get to walk into.

Now this transformation did not just affect this man. It affected the entire community. The people who saw him everyday as the lowly beggar now stand in awe and wonder! They praise God, they magnify him. They are captured by the greatness of his power and majesty! These events pointed to Jesus. No matter what they had heard no one could now argue with what they had seen with their eyes and people now had to decide how they would respond.

There are people in our worlds today, they are watching from the outside, they are looking at your life. They see your joy, your peace, the transformation in your life. They maybe see that job opportunity that has come out of the blue. They see that you were bound in depression and fear and now you are living with hope and a confidence about your future. They saw you crippled with pain and now they see you walking pain free. Whatever God has done in your life, choose to give it away. Share it with those around you. What you do have, give to them. Allow those streams of living water to flow through you and see Jesus transform the lives around you with his grace.

30

The Lord is always thinking about you!

*"*F*or I know the thoughts that I think toward you, says the LORD, thoughts of peace and not of evil, to give you a future and a hope."*

Jeremiah 29 vs 11

How do you feel when you know that someone is thinking of you? In a world that seems increasingly busy and with many people struggling to juggle the demands they face in life we are often surprised when people take the time to encourage us through an email or card or phone call out of the blue. For many of us we are living life at such a fast pace that we take little time ourselves to think about the direction of our lives. If we are not careful, we find ourselves so occupied with what's urgent that we often don't take the time to dwell on what is really important to us. Sometimes we can feel like we are stuck on a hamster wheel that just keeps turning. It can almost feel like a luxury to be able to press pause and to consider the bigger questions of life.

When we do get a minute to take time to dream about what could be we are often confronted by our shortcomings and our limitations. We all too easily allow mistakes from the past or fear of failure to quash any thoughts we might have of believing that life can be different from what we are currently experiencing.

Today you should take great comfort in the fact that the Lord is not short of time to think about where your life is going. He is not short of dreams for you. What is more he doesn't discount you for your failings, your inadequacies or insecurities. He only thinks good thoughts concerning you. Take a moment to let that sink in. It's hard for us to truly imagine what such unconditional love can look like. Even with the people we love the most, we can all at times disappoint each other and let one another down. Then we can find our thoughts towards each other becoming negative as we focus on the works of the flesh. But the Lord operates from an entirely different grid.

The Lord looks at you through the lens of his precious son Jesus. We understand that at the cross Jesus paid for every mistake and failing on our part. What we really need to get our heads around is the fact that when the Lord sees us, He sees the beauty and perfection of Jesus. He sees him spotless and blameless and it is with these same eyes that he chooses to see us.

In his perfect love He cherishes you and thinks only good thoughts about you. You can have hope for your future today because the God of all hope created you and placed you on this earth for a unique purpose. Each one of us is made in the image of God. Each one of us reflects his glory through our own special personality and gifting. That is why we can have confidence today for our tomorrows. This verse assures us that we are not only on the Lord's mind, but what he pictures when he thinks of us is goodness, blessing, favour, and the opportunity to reveal his glory.

The Lord has had his heart set on you for a long time. No matter how far you may feel you have strayed from the path the Lord has destined for you, remember today that He is the God of new beginnings, He is the Lord who restores the years the locusts have eaten and he is the Lord that has placed His living hope on the inside of you! Live today knowing that he goes before you. Don't let fear hold you back. He made you to be free, he made you for love, he made you fearless.

31

Conclusion

Our prayer is that over the course of these days you have been encouraged and built up to see life from a new vantage point. As a son or daughter of the King you can remain steadfast and hold on to the promises in the word and have a confidence about the future the Lord is leading you into. Fear is the devil's food so don't recognise it and cut it out of your diet. Instead feed on the Lord's love for you and allow his hope to shape your heart.

If you would like to find more resources that will help you thrive in life please connect with us through one of our social media platforms. You can connect via www.exchangechurchbelfast.com or visit Exchange Church on Youtube, Spotify, Facebook & Instagram.

About the Author

Penny has been involved in ministry for over 25 years. She currently lives in Belfast where she is married with 3 great kids. With her husband she founded Exchange Church Belfast, a church family that is committed to seeing the world transformed by the grace of God. She is a certified Executive Coach and facilitator working with some of the world's biggest brands providing leadership and management development programmes. A gifted speaker and leader, Penny uses her experience as a pastor, wife & mother to connect people to the truth of God's love and grace.

You can connect with me on:

🌐 http://www.exchangechurchbelfast.com

Subscribe to my newsletter:

✉ https://www.exchangechurchbelfast.com/devotional

Printed in Great Britain
by Amazon

87223376R00058